THE DEMISE OF THE CITY

OFF-GRID LIVING IN FAST CHANGING TIMES

THE DEMISE OF THE CITY

OFF-GRID LIVING IN FAST CHANGING TIMES

RHONDA BEYREIS

Tiny House and Rhonda's Dad.

I dedicate this book to my husband Jim Beyreis, who has always, and I mean always stood by me. Together with the Lord, we've made the Ark of Sustainability a reality on the Enoch Ranch. To my father, Dr John E. Alman, who took me on journeys as a child that impacted me and who believed in me and our mission. God rest his soul.

ACKNOWLEDGMENTS

I would like to thank Rainmaker Publishing for all their hard work and dedication to this finished project.

CONTENTS

Introduction 11
Identity Crisis and Survival
Chapter One 15
Growing Up Alongside A Hutterite Colony
Chapter Two 19
Never Going Back to Normal
Chapter Three 23
Money In the Wind
Chapter Four 29
The Era of Social Credit Scores and Vaccine Passports
Chapter Five 33
Dangers in the City
Chapter Six 43
Food and Supply Shortages
Chapter Seven 51
Raising and Growing Your Own Food
Chapter Eight 59
Down Grid/Cyber Attacks
Chapter Nine 67
Communication Down
Chapter Ten 73
Separation

Chapter Eleven   79
The Sick
Chapter Twelve   85
Community
Final Words   99
Rhonda is Available for Speaking   103
About the Author   104
Also by the Author   106
References   107

My people perish for lack of knowledge

—Hosea 4:6

INTRODUCTION

IDENTITY CRISIS AND SURVIVAL

I am a biracial Canadian who was adopted by white Americans when my biological mother left me in the hospital at birth.

I've been confused about my identity for most of my life. Black children would beat me up for not being "black enough," and white kids were just as mean. I didn't feel like I belonged anywhere.

Moving every four years between America and Canada didn't help.

In the 4th grade, my adoptive family moved to Texas, which was a significant culture shock. I struggled to fit in the Texan culture with all the accents and ways of life. And the spelling of words didn't help. Color in America is colour in Canada. Flavor in America is flavour in Canada. It was British rule.

They put me in special education classes to improve my language and spelling. That was completely humiliating as a 9-year-old, and I became self-conscious, thinking I wasn't smart enough.

When we moved to Iowa In 1976, things went from bad to worse. I hung out with the "misfits" who smoked cigarettes and pot, but I found solace in self-medicating to get through the school day.

My home life was full of abuse from a woman with schizophrenia, who couldn't control her hatred toward me. She was my dad's second wife, and her jealousy toward me only fueled my self-hatred.

Yet, despite all the hardships I went through at the beginning of my life, I learned how to survive. Dealing with abuse, loneliness, homelessness, legal troubles, and having nothing only meant the only place I could go was up.

I was introduced to the Lord during a stint in prison when my drug use backfired on me.

I have committed my life to serving my fellow man for the Lord ever since, especially those who are underdogs like I have been for most of my life.

I have walked alongside the mentally challenged, the homeless, the prisoners, and I have also been amongst the most wealthy. The greatest lesson I've learned from them all is that we are *all* God's children, and our blood runs the same.

I started looking at life differently in 1993 when I saw how crooked this world we live in really is. From courtrooms across the globe to the corrupt banking systems, living on grid is not the place to be during these times. I knew there had to be another way.

I started learning about living off-grid, first as a citizen of the city, and soon as a ranch owner who saw self sufficiency as the only way to survive.

Life isn't always fair, but we are chosen to walk the paths we are on. We learn from our mistakes and help others on their journeys and this book is me sharing my lessons and my journey with you.

As I see it, life is about to get even more challenging, and most people are oblivious to what lies ahead. We should not turn a blind eye to what's happening.

This is me looking at the future head on.

I will be sharing my personal stories and providing lessons learned, tips for survival, and resources to get you through troubled times.

This book by no means is meant to provide a complete strategy or comprehensive list of survivalist techniques. On the contrary, it is a taste to hopefully inspire you to want to learn more and to go out and seek it for yourself.

CHAPTER ONE

GROWING UP ALONGSIDE A HUTTERITE COLONY

I was in the kitchen cooking for a family of 10 most of my childhood. I learned at a very early age my way around a kitchen. My biggest chore was preparing breakfast for myself and my 7 siblings, 2 of which were adopted, like me, into the Alman family.

I would wake up early each morning, scramble eggs fresh off the farm, fry up salty bacon and toast crispy buttered bread before making a lunch sack for each sibling and seeing everyone off to school.

My father, Dr John E. Alman, was a large animal veterinarian and scientist.

At an early age, my dad began taking me with him to work. I was around five or six when he started working with the Hutterite community and we would go visit their farm that seemed more like a small, active city.

Different from Amish whose only industry was, at the time, single dairy farming, the Hutterites were a closed Anabaptist community in the provinces of Alberta and Manitoba. They lived on large, highly industrialized, communal farms and believed all material goods were community goods and that no one was too young or too old to play a part in taking care of the farm.

My family and I being allowed into the Hutterite's colony was unheard of. But my father, a talented veterinarian and scientist, was sought after by many farmers in North America. He would produce amazing animals, mostly hogs, that would be served at the table when the animals were ready for harvest. This impressed our Hutterite friends very much.

The community welcomed us with open arms. We played with their children, ate at their tables and slept in their feather beds when we went for our visits.

Seeing how their close-knit community was run always stuck with me. From how the women prepared the food in a huge kitchen and the younger men picked the food from the gardens, to how the elder men tilled the fields and tended to the large animals. What stood out most in my mind was seeing how, when food was prepared, all the men ate before the women and children.

Our visits to the Hutterite colony went on for about 4 years until my dad was called to Texas to start another set of farms and we had to move away to the United States.

Upon finding out about our departure, the Hutterites rallied around my dad, my siblings, and me, loaded us up with a huge baked turkey, bags of corn on the cob, and other goodies, and we said our goodbyes.

That divine appointment of being introduced to such a world at an early age gave me the courage as an adult to see things differently than what I had come to learn in my secular Canadian life. With the Hutterites, no one was left behind. Everyone had a job to do. From the young children to the elderly women and men, there was work to be done. They all added something of value to the community, and everyone was happy to do their part.

As I would come to learn in my own life, each role I saw around that farm would be crucial to the well-being of any community when the world comes to its most challenging times.

In 1977, our Hutterite friends came to visit us. We were living in Iowa, far away from our old life near the colony, but their visit brought all those memories of being on their land back to my heart.

I was reminded that no one person can do all things. We need each other. God has given each one of us gifts and talents. We all have the need to be needed, but we are also community minded, and well, we just need one another.

Though I did not love cooking breakfast and preparing sacks for me and my siblings, or preparing the evening meals, the upkeep on the house was the worst part of growing up. But I managed to turn what was upside down in my life into something great as an adult.

Today, one of my greatest gifts is cooking and entertaining people. I became a chef, a vegan chef at that.

ASK YOURSELF:

- What talents has God given you?
- How are those talents a benefit to your fellow man for the greater good of mankind?

CHAPTER TWO

NEVER GOING BACK TO NORMAL

The closer we get to the end of time, the more horrific the sinister acts of society are brewing. People do not want to believe that prophetic things are happening all around them. I hear people say, "things will go back to normal." "The government will save me." "Just make it all stop, and everything will be okay."

This is called Normalcy Bias. Normalcy Bias becomes amplified in troubled times and in populations where people or groups have lived with a minimal level of discomfort and resistance to the current realities.

The more minor this discomfort, the higher the level of normalcy bias one portrays. Most people will ignore or minimize threats of disaster specifically as far as how it affects them personally, usually out of some conscious or subconscious idea that 'They' won't let anything bad happen to me."

Well, it is happening to you. Just like the frog in the pot, it is coming at you in almost unnoticeable increments that are horrific. Riots, politics, murders, mandates, food and supply shortages, diseases, lockdowns, fake news, devaluation of the dollar, war and rumors of war. We—everyone of us on this planet—are a people under distress. Things are not going back to "normal." The world is angry. Life has changed and will continue to do so.

Biblically speaking, we can learn so much from the Good Book. The book of Matthew Chapter 24 tells such a story of the signs of these times and where we are today in earth's history:

> *"We are hearing of wars and rumors of wars: see that you are not troubled: for all of these things must come to pass, but the end is not. Nations will rise against nations, and kingdoms against kingdoms: and there shall be famines, pestilences, and earthquakes in diverse places. All of these are the beginning of sorrows."*

We can see on the global political field the horrors of wars and the talk of nuclear fallout. It seems like every time we turn around these days, The Ukraine, China, Russia, and the United States are on the main stage talking about or starting war. Geopolitical conflicts continue to rise.

We have seen firsthand how a global pandemic has changed the world. Lockdowns have occurred, people are dying, food and supplies are in shortage. During this time, fears have gotten out of control. Man is afraid of man. The News enhances our fears, causing more distrust. We truly are in crisis mode. Nothing is normal. People are in denial.

A house divided falls. We seem to slowly but surely continue to fall here in America.

Do you think we will ever go back to the way we used to be?

My friend, I am here to tell you. No. No, we will not.

CHAPTER THREE

MONEY IN THE WIND

When the dollar completely crumbles, it will be too late. The Central Bank Digital Currency (CBDC) will become full-fledged and you will no longer have the freedoms you have now. The CBDC is a digital form of a government-issued currency that isn't pegged to a physical commodity, such as gold, silver, etc. What this means is you will not only lose your privacy, but governments will use the CBDC as tools of financial discrimination. We currently see the expansion and destabilization of financial institutions, data breaches, and loss of security.

Mastercard, one of the primary forms of credit across the globe, has begun the process of pushing the CBDC to the forefront in America.

This is not just a rumble of 'maybe'. This train has already left the station.

There are 10 countries and territories with CBDCs and more than 100 others with projects in development. Active CBDCs are mostly in island countries: the Caribbean: Antigua, Jamaica, Barbuda, Saint Lucia, St. Kitts, Nevis and Dominica. But other active CBDCs include Nigeria–Africa's largest economy.

China, one of the world's largest economies, has started large-scale use of the E-yuan. According to Zenledger, one of the foremost sources of digital currency monitors, European officials are scheduled to launch their digital euro by 2025. America's

Federal Reserve is not far behind. The Bahamas's version, the "sand dollar," is already in circulation. The CBDC has begun in countries they know will accept this new deal.

We are all in for this undesirable treat. It is just a matter of when.

Central Bank Digital Currency has control of your finances according to "THEM" not you.

As you can see. 'They' have been setting up the cashless society for decades with credit cards, debit cards, your smartwatch pay, Zelle, PayPal, Venmo, online purchasing, e-commerce. The list of ways to pay cashless is astounding.

We are all affected by the CBDC's control in one fashion or another. Things are going to turn for the worst with the next phase of banking.

God said we will always have the poor. In my opinion, we are to help our fellow humans. When life goes completely cashless, how will we be able to help a struggling mother asking for help? Or a struggling individual looking for food?

I am notorious for handing a few dollars with some inspiring literature to those in need. Those opportunities will be over. I guess it is time to get creative and have extra toiletries, snacks and bottled water in our vehicles to continue to serve the poor.

Now is the time to get your preps in order. Buying and storing food. Purchasing land. Getting ammunition and purchasing firearms. Setting up solar so you're off the grid. Finding a community that is away from the system.

These things need to be in order now, because if you wait and this becomes live while you are still waiting, your window of opportunity will have closed.

I cannot express this enough. When this all goes down, you will not have the authorization from the authorities to get self sustainable because there will be a control of your finances, and of your entire life.

The Federal Reserve themselves are telling us that, beginning April 1, 2023, business pilots will begin. Then, beginning July, 2023, we will see a full-fledged target roll out for Central Bank Digital Currency in the United States.

The dollar is about to take a turn for the worst.

In China, citizens are only allowed to buy according to their carbon footprint and their good behavior. The country micromanages their people. This is called a social credit score and Americans are not far behind.

We will be so policed it will feel like there is no room to breathe. If you speak on what you see and feel and don't follow government protocol, you will be considered a danger to "THEIR" system and injustice will be served up.

We saw what happened to the Canadian truckers who stood their ground in 2022. Their Prime minister ordered their bank accounts to be frozen and they could not even get the fuel they needed. Good civilians came to the rescue with fuel and were arrested for their kindness.

That is part of "THEIR" agenda. Do not think this could not happen to you. Are we slaves to be told what to do and to be obedient?

The good book says: *"that no man might buy or sell, save he that had the mark, or the name of the beast, or the number of his name. [18] Here is wisdom. Let him that hath understanding count the number of the beast: for it is the number of a man; and his number is Six hundred threescore and six."*

CHAPTER FOUR

THE ERA OF SOCIAL CREDIT SCORES AND VACCINE PASSPORTS

Just like during the cold war times when people had to have papers to move around, we still must have our government issued documents to travel. First was your driver's license or ID card. Then a passport for international travel. Me being an immigrant—a green card—other immigrants need visas.

Today, in 2023, there is a new driver's license mandate that includes a star for travel. We used to worry about our credit score, but now there is talk of the new social credit score and vaccine passports. It seems like being an obedient citizen is becoming more like an invasion of privacy. 'They' will know who is compliant and follows the rules and those who are freethinkers and awake in nature. Can't you see what is really happening? Am I all alone in this?

As I go through the airport these days, they are sweeping everyone with dogs, just like when I was in South America. When I get to the counter to show my ID, 'They' are taking our pictures, just like 'They' do when I come in from other countries. This is the new system, and the only thing they are not doing at this time is fingerprinting us, but I can see that capability on the machine. Wake up, people. This is not normal. We have surveillance on every street corner in the city. The writing is on the wall; nothing is sacred anymore.

Look at your "Smart" TV, mandatory to have one, out with the analog one. You remember the one that couldn't listen in or watch you? Your smart TV is so smart that the camera on it can see what is happening in your home (mine is in a closed cabinet). The same goes for your computer, which can bring in and take out data. "Alexa" is a major home invasion; it's not as cute as you think it is!

Your camera doorbell ding-dongs as soon as it detects movement, and it starts recording. Rockwell recorded the song "Somebody's Watching Me" in

1984, released by Motown. Well, someone some-where really is watching you. Your movements will be on display for "Them" to see. 'They' are invad-ing your privacy!

> As Solomon says in Ecclesiastes 1:9, *what has been will be again, and what has been done will be done again; there is nothing new under the sun. The system has always invaded your privacy, but these days, it is on steroids.*

The system we grew up with has changed, and it is not on our side. I have firsthand experience with an unfair judicial system, crooked politicians, judg-es, and cops. I once sat in a courtroom with three people in the same situation, and they received dif-ferent judgments.

For 15 years, I was a bartender and often joined in after-hours parties where I witnessed doctors snorting cocaine before delivering babies, and a second-grade teacher once brought a briefcase full of drugs to a hotel room. Nothing seems sacred anymore.

Throughout my life, I've dated people from all walks of life. From the sons of vice presidents of major corporations and members of the CIA and DEA to party bums. I've seen so much, and things aren't what 'They' taught us they were supposed to be.

Biblically, famines, wars, rumors of wars, and pestilence are becoming more frequent. In society, what was once right is now considered wrong, and vice versa. This world is spiraling out of control.

During Hitler's day, the motto was "give them bread and circuses" (meaning entertainment). Today, people are becoming more selfish and lazy. As the government creates more chaos, they also create the solution that benefits only them. People are increasingly taught to be dependent on the government through stimulus checks and welfare.

A civil war between the haves and the have-nots is on the horizon.

When I go into the big city (which is not very often), I see gated communities pitted against each other. We are truly headed for disaster.

ASK YOURSELF:

- Is the government here to really save you?

CHAPTER FIVE

DANGERS IN THE CITY

The World Economic Forum and the Jesuit Order are believed to be among the organizations that control society from behind the scenes. They have established a hierarchy, wherein the easiest way to control people is through the services they need the most. This practice has been ongoing for decades, dating back to the creation of basic amenities such as the mercantile, the bank, the doctor's office, and the saloon in the early days. Today, with the addition of large-scale factory work, entertainment, and shopping, everything is conveniently accessible and available at one's fingertips.

As these sinister groups continue to pursue their agenda, they have now developed the concept of a smart city. According to Wikipedia, a smart city is a technologically modern urban area that uses electronic methods and sensors to collect specific data. This information is then used to manage assets, resources, and services efficiently, theoretically improving operations across the city.

At first glance, this may seem harmless. It may even seem useful. But these smart cities are utilizing your data that they collect from your devices as well as from buildings in your neighborhood. These assets are used to monitor and manage traffic and transportation systems in your community, along with the power plants, utilities, water supply networks, waste, criminal investigations, information systems, schools, libraries, hospitals, and other services that you, your family and your friends all rely on.

Smart cities are defined by both the ways in which their governments harness all of the technology used and how they monitor, analyze, plan, and govern the city with it. Data sharing is not limited to your city itself but includes your local businesses and third parties who can benefit from various uses of all of this data.

All of this smart city technology allows government city officials to interact directly with both community and city infrastructure and to monitor what is happening in your city. Whether you like it or not you are being monitored, spied on and sized up for *their* agenda. Many cities have already adopted some sort of smart city technology.

The **15-minute city** is an urban planning concept in which most daily necessities and services, such as work, shopping, education, healthcare, and leisure can be easily reached by a 15-minute walk or bike ride from any point in the city. This approach aims to reduce car dependency, promote healthy and sustainable living, and improve well-being and quality of life for city dwellers.

This also gives the government the chance to keep one big spying eye on every move you make.

This change in lifestyle may include remote working which reduces daily commuting and is supported by the recent widespread availability of information and communication technology (ICT). The concept has been described as a "return to a local way of life".

This is actually and simply the Demise of the City.

The concept behind these smart cities and 15-minute cities is the idea that a town or city can be designed so that pretty much all the stuff 'They' say you need in your daily life is no more than 15 minutes walk or cycle away in a certain grid or district and we will monitor you to make sure you comply. Your freedoms are being infringed upon. It is not if but when will these two ideologies merge together to complete the main part of their agenda. The smart city agenda was targeted in agenda 2030 as the time frame for these possibilities to be set in stone. History has shown us over and over again this type of tightening of society repress is never a good thing and this is going global. Nothing will be sacred, nothing will be the way we remember. We are pushing the rails into America the unknown. I have been witnessing this set up in the Phoenix, Arizona metro area for decades. In the 90's I could travel here, there and everywhere and see the exact same little strip malls which at the time I thought were pretty convenient. As we continue into 2018 things are getting a bit more wonky. All of the sudden the outdoor malls that have JCPenney, Marshalls, Ross, Home Goods, you know the type of mall have music in them now but the crazy thing is not the same music is playing out of all the speakers. Call me crazy but to me that is not normal, I see a holding center set up with different directive capabilities. Just wait and see. But for now, all your work, shopping, education, healthcare and leisure needs would be near where you live. The ideAIs to dramatically increase accessibility, as well as reduce your traffic and car usage –

essential to creating more environmentally-friendly societies. They have it all down, you will not leave your district because the powers at be, have put what 'They' say you need in a fifteen-minute gridlock and the means to monitor you to make sure you comply, or they can simply turn off your bank account. With society in their proper place, it is easier to control their subjects.

The concept behind smart cities and 15-minute cities is to design a town or city where all the essential services required for daily life are within a 15-minute walk or cycle in a specific grid or district. However, this ideas leading to excessive monitoring and loss of personal freedom. The merging of these two ideologies could complete the main part of *their* agenda. The smart city rollout is targeted in Agenda 2030 as the time frame for these actions to be implemented. History has shown that such tightening of society repression is never a good thing, and this trend is going global.

In the Phoenix, Arizona metro area, this setup has been ongoing for decades, with the same little strip malls present everywhere. The ideas that all your work, shopping, education, healthcare, and leisure needs would be within close proximity to your home, leading to increased accessibility and reduced traffic and car usage, thereby creating a more environmentally-friendly society.

However, some worry that this setup could be used to monitor and control individuals. They have it all down. You will not leave your district because the powers that be, have put what 'They' say you need in a fifteen-minute gridlock and the means to monitor you to make sure you comply, or they can simply turn off your bank account. With society in their proper place, it is easier to control their subjects.

Your community should be your first area of defense. I lived in a neighborhood in Phoenix where we made it a point to know our neighbors. The community had an old soul feel to it. During summertime, you can see each other walking and communicating with each other with a 'hello' and 'good morning' as one passes by.

I always walked my dogs in the morning along with other dog owners. We just knew each other. We created an email list to stay in touch and looked out for each other which came in handy when a crime spree would enter our community every so often until the criminals were caught.

Summer would bring in the Fourth of July Chili Cook-off and Christmas with luminary lights. We would all gather together to put sand in white paper bags along with real candles and hand out the luminary gifts to each home. Like with my Hutterite experience, no one was left out.

Christmas eve started with an animal parade after the luminaries were all put out on the curb and lit. We'd wander house to house gathering cookies, snacks or sipping on hot drinks. Just a tight knit community that made it a point to stick together.

I highly recommend you start to connect with your immediate community now so you are not a stranger when times of adversity arrive.

Starting a community garden is a great way to bring people together. While flowers are beautiful, food is a necessity, and a community garden can help address food insecurity in your community. By taking charge and initiating a community garden, you can promote interaction and cooperation among community members.

You could begin by organizing a get-together at your home, inviting everyone to participate in a potluck-style meal. This will encourage people to come together with a common purpose and engage with each other. Additionally, if there are water irrigation needs, you can collaborate to share resources and ensure that everyone has access to water.

Another way to involve more people in the effort is by encouraging everyone to grow food in their yards. By doing so, you can create a network of small-scale gardens that contribute to the community garden project. This will not only help to address food insecurity but also foster a sense of ownership and pride among community members.

In the cities there is pollution that creates health risks. In the city there is crime that puts unsettlement and stress into one's spirit. In these cities there are many mouths to feed and, as we are witnessing, a continual breakdown in the infrastructure of the city. As we move forward into the future, this will only push society to its breaking point.

What would a father do to provide for his hungry screaming child? Or a mother do for a sick family member? Normal people at the stress of the situation at hand will become villains in society. Get to know your neighbors to avoid the havoc. Civil unrest is inevitable. Be a good steward to prevent disaster in your community. The cities are a hotbed of mayhem and can truly be very dangerous.

Be solution minded.

COUNTRY LIVING

But alas, Ahhhh take a deep breath, a breath of fresh air. Look at the starry nights. Hey, look at the big dipper! And the beautiful landscape that can be seen for miles.

When 'the time' comes, you should make your way out of the city. We have gone through waves of opportunity to sell city dwelling to create a way out. You might just have to rent for a while, while you prepare. There are plenty of opportunities if you really want to move to country living. Buying an acreage with someone else to split is a more economical way, finding a like-minded community is another. God always has an answer for you. You say you cannot move because of your job? Well living out of the city you might just have to find another source or create a source of income like I did.

My husband and I have a 680-acre ranch that we've built an event space on while we are building a community for the future. Each day my husband and I find new ways to create sources of freedom to remove ourselves from under the hand of the government.

We have purchased commercial greenhouses to grow food as another source of income. Neighbors of ours raise chickens and sell eggs. Others sell bakery goods and soaps.

You could raise and sell chickens. You could create a microgreen business. You can take your skills and turn them into cash flow.

You will certainly have work to do, you just must find a niche market. There is always a need for a builder, a handyman and small engine and tractor repair people.

Sometimes you just must get creative.

The Good Book tells us in Revelations, "*And I heard another voice from heaven, saying, Come out of her my people, that ye be not partakers of her sins, and that ye receive not of her plaques. For her sins have reached unto heaven, and God hath remembered her iniquities.*'

We are to come out of the cities. I really don't think we were meant to live in them in the first place. As a child growing up mostly always living on a farm, I always wanted to live in the town so we could enjoy swimming pools, parks or movies. Little did I know at that time the benefits we had on the farm. Growing our own gardens which has come in handy in my adult life. Playing with animals. Climbing in trees. Swinging on the tree rope. Walking down railroad tracks. Having an imagination to create play time and to play hide and seek.

We knew when we went to town to go to the swimming pool or the skating rink it was a special time. It wasn't a time for video games to steal our joy and rob us of our imaginations.

I guess it really was a creative ok time.

CHAPTER SIX

A TISKET A TASKET WE LOST OUR LITTLE BASKET.

As you struggle to put food on the table for your family, it's hard not to worry about what other disasters may be on the horizon. The recent shortages of essential goods like eggs and baby formula serve as a stark reminder of just how vulnerable our supply chains can be.

But it's not just these specific shortages that we have to worry about. The world is facing an unprecedented number of supply chain disruptions, from shipping delays to factory shutdowns to labor shortages. And with the ongoing pandemic causing continued economic turmoil, the situation is only getting worse.

The government claims to be working to address these issues, but can we really trust them to take care of us? Or will they prioritize the interests of large corporations over the needs of ordinary citizens? It's becoming increasingly clear that we cannot rely solely on our leaders to solve these problems for us.

Remember the toilet paper shortage. Could you imagine what it will be like when there are canned goods shortages? Well, the way things are looking we will see canned food shortages in our lifetime. I believe the toilet paper shortage was a trial run, they saw what they needed to see. People's fears were raised, fights broke out, but no one was really injured in the toilet paper test. If it were jars of pasta sauce or cans of tuna there would have been cleanup in aisle 7.

As food and supply shortages become more commonplace, we must take matters into our own hands. This means supporting local businesses, growing our own food, and being prepared for the worst. It's a daunting task, but the alternative is a future where our basic needs are not being met, and our government is unable or unwilling to help us.

CHANGES IN OUR SCHOOL SYSTEM

In 1994 the educational system took basic skills out of the school curriculum with the excuse being "unavailable funding." I remember in middle school—or Junior High as we called it—starting basic skills classes. Home economics, which was cooking, sewing and the basics of keeping the home. Then there were pottery and wood burning classes. Moving into High School there were auto mechanics and shop classes.

The decision was made to eliminate trade skills and direct students into a college mentality which would bring more money to the system causing financial hardship to students and their families for long periods of time. This would fill "Their" pockets and put a whole lot of people into a new kind of debt.

We can look at society today and see we have lost the skill sets needed to survive. Basic skills. The ability to do basic skills around the home has really gone out the window. People would rather be on their devices than plant a garden. We have been programmed into another direction, and it is time to hone back in on those basic skills. This will be life changing.

I challenge you to teach yourself, and, if you have children, teach your children to sew, cook, or plant a single herb and teach them to nurture their herb and harvest it.

Something happens to a person when they can see the fruits of their labor. This also brings families together. Spend quality outside time with your family. Take a walk. Walk the dog. Play ball. All of these are outside activities. Try something other than being on your monitored device.

THE SLEEPING DOG

WE ARE A DEPENDENT, LAZY GENERATION, WITH LUXURIES all around us to our demise. Our grandparents and great grandparents knew how to work the fields, grow and preserve food, make medicine, raise animals, pour soap as well as design, sew, and fix clothing.

Where has all the talent, wisdom, and knowledge gone? Mostly to the grave. This fact could be the death of many people who rely on the government and the system to save them. Over the years, we have become complacent in our own minds, thinking that someone else will save us, as we have been trained to do. However, it is up to us to stand strong and save ourselves. But how can we do this when essential skills have been ignored throughout the ages, and a life of ease has been served up on a silver platter?

I will tell you how. Get with it while you still can! Join an online gardening club or seek out a community garden in person. Stop wasting your time binge-watching Netflix and start moving. Be mindful today for the destruction of tomorrow. Let's be real, 'They' certainly have shown us in plenty of movies how "they " control the system.

MOVIES: FACT OR FICTION?

I RECALL A MOVIE IN WHICH A GROUP OF WEALTHY INdividuals sat atop their dwelling, tossing food and water down to the impoverished while they observed the poor people battling each other for sustenance, all for their amusement.

I am sure you can recall a similar situation in a movie. The crazy thing is the movies have desensitized the masses because the movie industry—who are a part of the system, by the way– tell you years in advance what is going to happen. Everyone sits in movies to be entertained. I encourage you next time you sit in a movie, put on your investigative goggles and ask yourself what are they really telling me?

There is always an underlying message for you. There are several documentaries on social credit scores. Netflix's "Black Mirror" from 2017. Streaming right now as a new release is the movie "Inside" where an individual is locked inside an art vault and goes crazy. Sound familiar? How about the recent global lockdowns that made people stir crazy and what these individuals escalated to?

We are being programmed through social media, movies, fake news and through the group thinking of the masses. Be open minded. Look around at what you see, hear and allow into your mind. Is it real? Or is it part of an agenda they want you to accept as real?

Artificial Intelligence (AI) is also taking over the scene. Right now the hottest topic is ChatGPT. This is teaching the masses to trust and use AI as a means of writing, publishing and making copy. We have already seen the abuse of this in photo shopped content.

What will this escalate to? Having the app on your device is inviting AI into your world. You don't even have to think anymore. The device will do all the thinking for you. I don't know about you, but I see this as a danger in the future. Machines should be in the service of human beings not human beings in the service of machines.

If we can allow autonomous weapons to deploy and engage with their own targets, we certainly will see proportionate false fatalities. We have all seen the Boston Dynamics robots on social media or the television at one time or another. These are life sized robots, some in the figuration of a four-legged animal totally equipped with the capabilities of taking out their targets. Others are in the shape of a human. We have all seen movies where AI has taken over and eliminated their targets, the humans who think for themselves. I believe that this too will become a reality.

Look at the older movies with the robots taking over humans, attacking and them hunting down. We truly are on the verge of the known and unknown.

The movie industry has also been showing this to us over and over again in the movies. If you really want confirmation on how things have been shown to us, the movie Terminator and Matrix series can put it all into perspective for you. "Soylent Green," is another movie produced in the early 70's—1973 to be exact—and it correctly shows how the world has progressed up to the year 2022. The story line tells the decline and manipulation of "THEM" against humanity and only the rich have meat, jam, alcohol and the finer things in life. The masses are eating man made food and have a need for the newest food on the market. This movie shows homelessness, despair, and the decline of the human race. Those that are picked for government policing have some freedom to move around. There is curfew, lockdowns. Sound familiar?

They also show self-surrender suicide. The suicide pod really did come out in the year 2022 in Switzerland. If you are depressed or your body doesn't function at full capacity, you can legally self-surrender suicide in Canada now. Do you realize that the system started promoting the climate change agenda offering manmade foods, skyrocketing the meat, eggs and dairy in 2022? Pretty soon the rich will be the ones enjoying the finer things in life as the rest will be told what they can and cannot have. We are on a fast-pace train track heading for disaster.

Open your eyes and take a good look at where we are today. Do you not get it? 'They' tell you everything in the movies to desensitize you. Hmmm, I have seen this before. And you sure have, too! Pay attention.

It is imperative for you to purchase the things you need to survive today because tomorrow the dollar could be 100% gone and supply could be depleted. I say that <u>definitively</u>.

I hear all the time that I am over the top ridiculous. I am okay with that.

CHAPTER SEVEN

RAISING AND GROWING YOUR OWN FOOD

THE BASIS OF SELF—SUSTAINABILITY

FRESH PRODUCE

THE TENDER LOVING CARE OF PLANTING—FROM SEEDling, nurturing, watering and watching it grow into a sustainable food source—just does something to one's soul. So satisfying. Vine ripened fresh picked tomato. Just one bite. Nothing like it!

Turn those tomatoes into fresh salsa or marinara sauce… delicious! The nutritional value…amazing!

Questioning whether it is or isn't really organic is out the window. It _is_ organic!

Raising and growing your own food is essential for self-sustainability, especially in a world that is facing an uncertain future. It's important to start where you are, and you can begin with something as simple as a windowsill herb garden. Even a plastic clamshell from the grocery store can be repurposed as a mini greenhouse to start your seedlings. If you have a patio and live in an apartment, try growing plants like lettuce, Swiss chard, or tomatoes in pots. Adding food to your flower garden is another great way to start.

Knowing about edible weeds is also important. Plant them away from your regular garden so that you have a source of nutrition if your garden is pilfered while you are away or sleeping. It's surprising how many plants that we consider weeds are actually edible and nutritious. You just need to know which ones to choose.

Growing medicinal plants is also a great idea. As the need for home doctors increases, having access to medicinal plants will become more important. Onions, turmeric, ginger, garlic, and capsaicin peppers like cayenne or jalapeño peppers are all excellent choices for a healing garden. There are teas that heal and teas that calm, and plants like aloe vera and cabbage have specific healing properties as well.

If you live in a climate that allows citrus to grow, consider planting lemons and grapefruit. Starting a beehive is another great way to promote pollination and have a source of honey. The possibilities for growing your own food and medicine are endless, and having an Herbalist or Naturopath on your team is golden. So start small and keep learning, and soon you'll be well on your way to self-sustainability.

SAVE IT FOR A RAINY DAY

FOOD PRESERVATION

THERE IS NOTHING LIKE HOME GROWN FOOD AND PUTting it up for the winter or a rainy day by canning, dehydrating, freeze-drying or salt drying just like our grandparents used to do.

In modern times, we can grow food all year round with greenhouses. All of these ways of food preservation will prove to be helpful in times of food shortages, and we have food storages.

Storing your dry goods in the proper container like flour and sugar for long term storage is a must. Flour bags don't come in sealed bags which often in long term storage can create a problem if not attended properly. I take my bag of flour, wrap it well in a couple of plastic grocery sacks, and freeze the flour for at least 3 days. The grocery sacks keep ice crystals from forming on the outside of the flour sack which would cause moisture in your flour. Upon taking the flour out of the freezer I dump it into a large bowl where I add food grade Diatomaceous Earth. Then I store my flour in heavy plastic bags and put them into Gamma Vittle Vaults.

Sugar needs to be kept in a sealed container as well. 5 gallon food grade buckets with the gamma lid works great to keep out pests.

Recipe: ½ C Food Grade Diatomaceous Earth to 20 lbs of flour.

I am a stickler for dehydrated foods and freeze-dried foods. They also need to be stored properly. I store all my prepared foods with oxygen absorbers. It is the simple things that truly make the difference. I have dehydrated just about everything. I use my freeze dryer especially for things I can not dehydrate, like sauces, desserts, liquid foods. I cannot tell you how important it is to get started in your preparations now.

Someone is counting on you!

Hardtack is another sustainable food source that can be made stored properly and can feed your family for years to come. Hardtack is a food that lasts 25 years or more if stored properly, making it the perfect emergency survival food. Historically Soldiers were known to survive for months on end, almost entirely on Hardtack.

REFERENCE: https://www.deliciouscooks.info/civil-war-hardtack-recipe

HERE ARE SOME ADDITIONAL THINGS TO DO FOR FOOD preservation and preparing your cupboards during difficult times:

1. **Canning** - This is a great way to preserve fruits and vegetables, and it can be done at home with a pressure canner or water bath canner. This method seals the food in an airtight container and can last for years.
2. **Pickling** - Pickling is a process of preserving food in an acidic solution such as vinegar. It can be done with vegetables, fruits, and even eggs.
3. **Fermenting** - Fermenting is a process of breaking down sugars in food by bacteria, yeasts, or other microorganisms. It can be used to preserve vegetables and fruits, and it also has numerous health benefits.
4. **Smoking** - Smoking is a process of preserving food by exposing it to smoke from burning wood or other materials. It adds flavor and can be used for meats, fish, and cheese.

5. **Root Cellaring** - This is a method of storing root vegetables such as potatoes, carrots, and beets in a cool, dark, and humid environment. This can extend their shelf life for several months.

6. **Using Food Grade Buckets** - These buckets can be used for storing bulk dry goods such as rice, beans, and flour. They are airtight and can be stacked, making them ideal for long term storage.

7. **Using Oxygen Absorbers** - These are packets that remove oxygen from a container, preventing the growth of bacteria and fungi. They are often used in combination with food grade buckets for storing dry goods.

8. **Hardtack** - As mentioned earlier, hardtack is a type of hard bread that can last for decades if stored properly. It is an excellent source of sustenance during emergencies or survival situations.

Food preservation and proper storage are essential for ensuring a sustainable food source during difficult times. Whether it is canning, dehydrating, smoking, or storing dry goods, taking the time to prepare now can make all the difference in the future.

HEN IN THE HEN HOUSE

Eggs in the city are up to $10 a carton! This is ridiculous!

In the US, eggs already have a short shelf life due to being washed. Egg producers with 3,000 or more laying hens must wash their eggs with methods that include using soap, enzymes or chlorine. The idea is to control salmonella that can cling to eggs.

But in other countries, eggs are left on dry shelves, not in the refrigerated section of the grocery store.

Chickens running around… fresh farm eggs… Priceless.

I had a chicken as a pet on our farm in Phoenix AZ. Her name was Chick-a-Chicken. She would run to me and go for walks on the farm then snuggle with me.

Chickens make great pets. They eat bugs and leave behind fertilizer for a healthy garden. They also provide eggs for families to eat.

Their fresh eggs can be glassed* providing a shelf life up to 18 months.

(Here is a recipe for glassing eggs provided by the blog, Farmhouse on Boone) https://www.farmhouseonboone.com/water-glassing-eggs

Remember when I shared that my dad was a Veterinarian? I learned a lot having him as my dad.

I learned early that there are many benefits to having farm animals. Not only does it promote character as one learns animal husbandry, but having the ability to have large animals with room to roam is an undeniable blessing.

Seeing my two horses run by, hearing my neighbor rancher's cow moo, and the cock crow, beats the blaring sounds of sirens from police cars, ambulances and fire trucks in the city.

CHAPTER EIGHT

DOWN GRID/CYBER ATTACKS

BABY IT'S DARK OUTSIDE

Grid down. The desperation of a power grid going down will bring on a whole other can of worms to your demise. If the grid goes down and the power across the city goes out, your survival preparation and your purchasing ability comes to a halt.

Have you ever noticed that when your power goes out your water doesn't work? When the grid goes down, there will be no water that can be pumped from to the taps for drinking, bathing, washing or flushing. This means sewage will become a problem bringing on health issues.

I recommend you have an additional supply of kitchen garbage bags and plastic grocery sacks in your preps for waste refuse. This will become your portable toilet and keep things sanitary.

Life becomes dark. Not only physically, but the challenges associated with a down grid affect us in so many ways. ATMs won't work. If you do not have cash on hand, your life stops. Credit and debit cards won't work and cash will only be accepted for a little while as those who have it frantically run to the pharmacy to get their medicine or to the grocery store for food and preps. This will go on until the store is empty or the store owner is robbed.

If you think I am exaggerating, just look at all the mayhem when our world experienced a global pandemic.

The supply chain will end as the last drop of fuel is squeezed out of fuel tanks and delivery trucks come to a screeching halt.

SOLDIERS IN THE MAKING

The Good Book says: *"And when you see Jerusa-lem surrounded by armies, then you will know that the time of its destruction has arrived."*

BY NOW THE TEMPERS OF MEN ARE OUT OF CONTROL. It is a me-me situation. What will it take to get what I need to serve my family and the family pets? What is yours is mine and what's mine is mine.

The food is scarce. Makeshift militia (thugs) band together in hopes of gathering supplies from those they can take from. *Oh look I see a light, let's go!* It is a struggle, it is a fight, the thugs are stronger; they are many.

We take our loss and move on. Only the strong hold the line. Soon the strong find the strong; pooling their resources together. Now it is *them* against *us*. These militant groups continue on like a Mad Max movie. We saw this, too during the pandemic.

THE TOILET PAPER SCARE

DURING THE TOILET PAPER SCARE, PEOPLE WERE LITER-ally beating each other up over toilet paper. This experiment totally played itself out. 'They' in my opinion created the shortages, then 'They' filled the shelves. Micromanaging the toilet paper created the scarcity. There were long lines, fights, and angry people. Can you imagine what it would have been like in this experiment if it was canned goods?

Just imagine. That time is coming. Your best bet is to gather as you go. Buy a little extra preps as you make your weekly trips to the store. Keep an eye on your preps, rotate your foods so you do not waste any. Think about some things you can use for barter and trade. Laundry soap, medicine, beef jerky, coffee, water, food, ammo, alcohol for distillation, make tinctures, even socks.

When you travel, always collect the little hotel soaps, shampoos and conditioner samples. They will certainly come in handy. There are other items that will come in handy, too.

Seeds. I believe seeds will be the poor man's currency. There is life in seeds. You can eat seeds. Chia seeds were the seeds that sustained the Mayan culture. It was called running man's seed. Chia grows so easily. Remember the chia pet? You would soak the chia seed, creating a gel then you brush the chia gel on the ceramic Obama head and hair would grow. It is that easy. Chia is part of the sage family, the beautiful flowers provide nectar for bees and butterflies. Not only are its seeds edible, so are the leaves. Starting your organic Non-GMO seed bank will prove to be one of the smartest preps you can acquire, not just for food but for trade.

HERE IS A LIST OF OTHER ITEMS THAT WILL COME IN HANDY:

1. **Water:** This is the most important item to have in any emergency situation. You should have at least one gallon of water per person per day.

2. **Food:** Non-perishable food items like canned goods, dried fruits, and nuts can be helpful in emergencies.

3. **First Aid Kit:** A well-stocked first aid kit with bandages, antiseptic ointment, pain relievers, and other essentials can be crucial in emergencies.

4. **Shelter:** Emergency blankets, tents, and sleeping bags can help protect you from the elements.

5. **Tools:** A multi-tool, a knife, a flashlight, and a radio can be useful in various emergency situations.

6. **Personal hygiene items:** As mentioned above, soap, hand sanitizer, toilet paper, and feminine hygiene products should be included.

7. **Cash:** It is important to have some cash on hand in case electronic payment systems are not functioning.

8. **Important documents**: Keep copies of important documents such as passports,

IDs, and insurance policies in a water-proof container.

9. **Medications:** Keep a supply of any necessary medications or medical supplies.

10. **Means of self-defense**: In the event of a mass global attack, some people may consider firearms or other means of self-defense. However, it is important to remember that such items should be handled responsibly and legally.

SOLAR OFF—GRID LIVING

SMALL SCALE COMFORTS

YOU HAVE THE LUXURIES OF BEING SUSTAINABLE TODAY like never before. Investing today for tomorrow is one of the smartest things you can do for yourself and your loved ones.

I recently invested in my son's family. I gifted them a Bluetti solar generator with extra panels to provide them with peace of mind if the grid goes down. A solar generator is soundless opposed to a gas generator that screams, "here we are, we have preps!"

Think outside the box. "What if" should be your go-to motto. My son has two children and a nursing wife, so a practical gift just seemed better to be proactive. Assessing yours and your loved one's situations could be the matter of life and death. A solar generator with the capacity to run your refrigerator and small appliances such as a cell phone and laptop or lamp, can keep a family up and going.

Do your research wisely. Not all solar generators are alike.

Another solar prep is putting solar on your house. Not having the correct information will have one buying into solar that is controlled and managed through the electric company. Well guess what? You are still connected to the grid. 'They' still have control over your power. The best way to connect to off-grid solar is just that. Do not connect to the powers that be. You need to have your own solar panels and inverter and your own batteries. A system you control, not that the electric company controls.

We upgraded our whole solar system to Sol-Ark here on The Enoch Ranch. We have the top of the line off-grid system. We are the bougie Survivalists!

But you don't need to be. You should at least have a solar generator and a few panels. There are many brands out there. You need to do your homework. Not all systems are the same. We also purchased Eternalight which is a light bulb to place into any light fixture and when the power goes out the internal battery of the Eternalight will be charged. If a power outage does occur the Eternalight will automatically power on providing up to 6 hours of battery powered illumination.

There are many simple ways to bring back everyday comforts in an emergency. These are a few of mine. I am always looking for alternatives. I am always looking for answers. You too should find alternatives that will hold the tide in this game called life.

CHAPTER NINE

PHONE DOWN

Hello, hello is anybody out there? Does anybody have any service? I have no bars.

How will you find your loved ones during an emergency if your cell phone is down? Where is Mary? If the grid goes down, we are in trouble. First water. now cellular.

We are on the verge of something catastrophic. Who created the smart Bomb, afterall? America did, that's who. Again, if you don't believe, just look around. It's right in front of all of our eyes. Maybe your eyes are just closed.

Without tele-communication there is no way to immediately tell if your family is ok.

You need a step-by-step clear plan.

STEP 1: ESTABLISH A MEETING PLACE

IN THE EVENT THAT TRADITIONAL FORMS OF COMMUNI-cation are down, it is important to have a designated meeting place where family members can regroup. This can be a specific location within your community, or a landmark that is easy to find.

STEP 2: DESIGNATE A PRIMARY CONTACT

SELECT A PRIMARY CONTACT PERSON THAT FAMILY members can communicate with to exchange information about their whereabouts and any other pertinent information. This person should have a reliable means of communication, such as a two-way radio, satellite phone, or other form of communication that is not dependent on traditional communication networks.

STEP 3: IDENTIFY ALTERNATIVE FORMS OF COMMUNICATION

IDENTIFY ALTERNATIVE FORMS OF COMMUNICATION that can be used in the event that traditional forms are unavailable. Some examples include two-way radios, CB radios, satellite phones or ham radios.

STEP 4: CREATE A FAMILY EMERGENCY PLAN

CREATE AN EMERGENCY PLAN WITH YOUR FAMILY MEMbers that outlines what to do in the event that traditional forms of communication are unavailable. This should include information on how to reach the designated meeting place, as well as any other necessary information such as emergency contact numbers, medical information, and so on.

Having your designated meeting place is crucial. If Joey is over at Mable's house playing with Little Carter, Carter's family needs to be on the same prep plan as your family.

The clock has started, your friends have all agreed to the meeting times and places. You are on the same mission to weather the storm together.

Imagine: The countdown started. You only have from now up to 2 hours to arrive at your first family designated meeting place. If you can't make it, you must decide to go to the second place where you have 4 hours to arrive at meeting place number two. Get moving so you don't get left behind. In times of trouble, most people will not have preps or a meet up plan. Make sure those you are involved with understand your plan. It might mean having to close up your contacts. Your community may get smaller. Having a structured game plan will give you and your family peace of mind because a plan is in place.

REFERENCES: https://www.airuniversity.af.edu/Portals/10/ASPJ/journals/Chronicles/apjemp.pdf

HAM AND CB RADIOS

BREAKER-BREAKER ONE NINE

ALTERNATIVE COMMUNICATION WILL BE A MAJOR BLESSing in these times of uncertainty. Having a battery-operated weather radio will bring in some sort of outside communication. Being equipped with just a handheld CB radio will certainly bring in hand to hand local communication. You should invest now in a $20-$30 handheld CB radio on Ebay that will power up in your 12 volt port in your vehicle or plug into the wall.

A home base station will also bring comfort of communication on a short distant stent. On a more global scale, having a Ham Radio will be the most effective source of communication as one can receive information and communicate with loved ones around the world. You need a license to be an active Ham Radio technician speaking freely on day-to-day communication. You can study the book and pass your test and be one of many on the airways. I encourage you to do it. There is so much to learn from so many people and Hams, as they call it, really are good ole folk. Always helpful in sounding the alarm in a time of danger. Giving a helping hand in a time of need. Even if you don't have a license it is good to have a base station today and get your license tomorrow. Do not let a license intimidate your preps and stop you. Keep prepping!

CHAPTER TEN

SEPARATION

At some point during a fallout, you may very well be separated from those who you count on and love. One of the most important things you can do during this kind of crisis if you're separated from your family, is not stand out like Bambi, or like a sore thumb.

The first thing to always keep in mind is Stay Calm and Think Clearly. Panic and confusion can lead to poor decision-making, which can make the situation worse. Take a deep breath and try to assess the situation objectively.

Unlike what we're taught today, you will want to blend in and be unnoticeable. Take off expensive jewelry, designer clothing or any items that make you stand out. All that will do for you is attract the wrong kind of people. You will need to fit in as much as possible.

If you are home and the thugs are headed your way and your house looks to not be broken into, get out and scatter stuff on your lawn and become invisible. If you are on foot, move with the crowd until you can get into a safer environment. Become an actor or actress whichever scenario you find yourself in. Your life is at stake and your loved ones need you.

You need to become as much a part of this landscape as you can until you can find your family. Always keep an eye on your surroundings and be very mindful of the one who seems to be in charge. Be helpful and get them to respect you as you give as much respect as you can back. Remember you are the actor. Pay attention to those who are trustworthy. Be careful who you confide in. Everyone really is on the take, trying to make it through. If it means their life or yours, well I think we both know who they will take care of so be helpful and mindful.

Do not be the whiny cry baby that is a burden to the group because you will be taken out of the group. You bring no value to the table and your extra winey mouth is too expensive to feed. So be pro-active in this delicate situation.

CREATE YOUR ESCAPE ROUTE

BEING IN THE CITY YOU SHOULD MAP OUT YOUR ESCAPE route. Look around at how the freeways are structured. I have watched the city of Phoenix, Arizona grow into the monstrosity they are today. I watched the second then the third, fourth and finally the fifth freeway systems come in. What most people see is convenience. What I see is 'They' finally wrapped the whole city into a connective freeway system which, if needed, the military can prevent the people from leaving the city.

But because I have always been a loophole seeker I found one way out. That's me! If I ever get stuck in Phoenix during this time, that loophole still exists to this day and I will be able to exit.

You really need to look around your city and find an exit plan, you really do not know when you will need one. It is better to be prepared now than to wish you could have or should have.

Be proactive, someone is counting on you.

GO BAG — WE GOT IT ALL, DOLL

IN THE TIME OF INTENSE TROUBLE WHEN THERE SEEMS to be no hope, it is time to move. You cannot take your entire house with you. This is the time to grab and go. You need to have your grab-and-go preparations far in advance. And, as always, you need to think out of the box.

That goes for everyone in your family. Just because I am a mom does not mean I can carry everything for my kids on my back. It is time to get little Johnny his own backpack with his own favorite little toys and a clean outfit, and make a game out of it. Practice wearing your packs, so everyone understands their own go bags and the importance of them.

What really is your Go or Bug-Out Bag? This is a grab and go bag or pack that has the essentials of at least three days, 3 weeks, or until things get back to stable or manageable times. Your go bag is full of your preps for what most people identify as doomsday. When it comes to carrying your preps, you need to be mindful not only of the contents but also the weight. Here are a few suggestions for your go bag that certainly can be elaborated on.

- Flashlight
- Compass
- Fire Started
- Water Purifier of some sorts (I use a Life-Straw)
- Water bottle
- Warm Clothing

- Tarp for shelter can collect water
- Sleeping Bag
- MoleSkin for blisters
- A Good Knife
- Hatchet
- Army Folding Shovel
- Twine or Paracord
- Medical Pocket Book
- Band-Aids
- Antibiotic Cream
- Bug Spray
- Prescriptions
- Money
- Your Important Papers
- Food
- Cooking Utensils

You more than likely have your mind spinning on all of the things you need to add to this list just like I did. As a matter of fact, I huffed that FULL pack on my back, and I realized only the items that were going to save me and my family in this time of need were the most important. I had to take a good look at comfort to survive, and there is a difference. I can now manage my pack.

Speaking of packs, The right kind of pack is important. A school book bag backpack is not going to give you the support you need for long journeys.

Choosing to go to your local sporting goods store and getting fit for a pack that is weight bearing and has a good waist and back support is not a waste of your time. You will be thankful over and over again. All the comforts from home are nice but let's be real.

CHAPTER ELEVEN

THE SICK

In chaos and troublesome times, whether it is a pandemic or some other catastrophe, there will always be sick people. More people than usual will need medical attention during this time due to the circumstances.

With the lack of medication and the demand for help, the hospitals will be short staffed which will cause its own kind of panic. People's emotions will be raised to fear and anguish. Individuals in the medical field also have their own families to care for.

There just is not going to be enough medicine or staff to go around.

In this case, I have a survival hack. You can purchase antibiotics from an animal feed store in the fish section. Fish Mox (amoxicillin), Fish Pen (penicillin), Fish Biotic (cephalexin) for example. You're welcome.

Prep your medicine supplies now.

- Antibiotic cream
- Peroxide
- Bandages
- Suter Bandages
- Campho-Phenique
- Rubbing Alcohol
- Aspirin
- Tylenol
- Castor Oil
- Vicks Vapor Rub
- Bacterin
- Baby Powder
- Toothbrush
- Toothpaste
- Tooth pain kit
- Bar soap

This list can certainly be elaborated on. These are just a few ideas of some of the more generic things you can or should stock up on.

NATURAL REMEDIES

WHAT IF YOU ARE NOT ABLE TO GET TO A MEDICAL FAcility? There is still hope for you. Nature has its own way of healing. Medicine always starts first with plants.

Learning your way around the garden will help you know which plants do what for what ailment.

- The willow tree bark is good for headaches and fevers.
- Cabbage wrapped around a sprain heals inflammation.
- Potatoes pull out infection.
- Warm onion draws out ear infections.
- Nature's Flu Shot see recipe in back of book) is full of antimicrobials, anti-biotic, anti-bacterial, and antiseptic properties

Here is a list of other natural remedies:

1. **Ginger:** Ginger has anti-inflammatory and pain-relieving properties. It can help relieve nausea, vomiting, and headaches. You can take ginger in various forms like ginger tea, ginger ale, or simply chewing a small piece of fresh ginger.

2. **Honey:** Honey has antibacterial and anti-inflammatory properties. It can help soothe a sore throat, cough, and cold.

You can take honey directly or mix it with warm water or tea.

3. **Eucalyptus oil:** Eucalyptus oil has antiviral, antibacterial, and decongestant properties. It can help relieve nasal congestion and cough. You can inhale eucalyptus oil by adding a few drops to hot water and inhaling the steam.

4. **Garlic:** Garlic has antibacterial and antiviral properties. It can help boost the immune system and fight infections. You can consume garlic in various forms like eating it raw, adding it to food, or taking garlic supplements.

5. **Aloe Vera:** Aloe Vera has anti-inflammatory and antibacterial properties. It can help soothe skin irritations and burns. You can apply aloe vera gel directly to the affected area.

6. **Chamomile:** Chamomile has anti-inflammatory and sedative properties. It can help relieve anxiety, stress, and promote sleep. You can drink chamomile tea or use chamomile essential oil for aromatherapy.

Your pharmacy truly comes from the garden. There are so many remedies for modalities. I recommend finding a pocket book on Amazon and keeping it with your pack.

CHAPTER TWELVE

COMMUNITY

BRING IT BACK HOME

As much as I learned throughout the years about survival due to my circumstances of life, one of my greatest lessons was that we still need each other.

When I say I attended the 'school of hard knocks', I left home at 15 because of abuse, put my-self through high school while living on my own, had a job that supported me and yet, through all of this, I still managed to graduate with my graduating class.

Though today I have created a life I love, life has not always been easy for me. I walked away from a dysfunctional family and many times I felt all alone. I managed to move all around the country. From the midwest to the west. I even ended up in Hawaii for a year. Through it all, I managed to create friendships in my travels along the way.

There really is nothing like a community. Life just seems more serene when one knows they are not all alone, and you have someone you truly can count on. As much as I have learned throughout the years of surviving life's circumstances, it is clear that we still need each other. We will always need each other.

Just like the Hutterite's Colony, an Off-Grid Community, there are so many jobs to be done and a lone wolf just cannot do them all, all the time. Eventually there is going to be a season of sickness and the lone wolf is going to need help from others.

It's time to find yourself a community of people you can really trust. A community of like-minded people. Make sure you know what you are getting into. Are they a group of Bible believing people, or are they Militia type? Is the group you are looking for only sharing the land, or do they also share the work and have similar ethics and values? Is this your blood family or community-family? You need to be clear on what you are looking for. It would be good for you to go visit the community you are looking to join before making any final decisions.

THE ENOCH RANCH COMMUNITY — THE ARK OF SUSTAINABILITY

IN 2005, JIM—MY HUSBAND OF ALMOST TWENTY years—and I stepped out and answered the call from the Lord. For five straight years, while Jim worked in the United States, I traveled around the world doing mission work looking for the place we were to set up for the Lord. The place we would call, not only *our* home, but a community for others.

We knew we were called but had no idea where we were to be. Working steadily on our efforts, God brought us right where we are in N.E. Arizona to a property that He told me, in a very audible voice as we drove with the realtor onto the property, "this is the land I saved for you."

We looked more intensely at it than at any other property shared with us and this land had every criteria we were looking for. God is faithful! He has provided thus far.

In 2010, 680 acres, what we now call "Enoch Ranch", was purchased. It had an old solar system, a couple of wells, a few buildings including one built into the earth, a working shop, a single-wide and plenty of empty land.

Today, fast forward to 2020 "The Ark of Sustainability" is a thriving community.

We've upgraded and remodeled our solar system, put in a solar well, remodeled the mobile home into a commercial kitchen, put up single yurts and tiny homes, and we've only just begun. We have big plans here.

We use our skills and the skills of others to train those who are looking to also learn how to become self-sustaining.

Yurt building shows how easy it is to erect a home.

There is nothing like knowing how to garden and how to put up a harvest.

We have found solutions to solar and alternative communication.

Knowing how to start a fire and being able to create a debris shelter in a pinch is an excellent skill to have.

Understanding and knowing how to use firearms so you are not afraid of them is a bonus.

There could, one day, be a time when we must leave this all behind and head out on foot with a grab and go bag. But we are ready to go in this type of emergency. And we find pleasure in helping others be ready as well.

We do not know what the future holds, but what we do know here at the Enoch Ranch is one can never be too prepared.

We are a training facility that helps individuals understand off-grid living. But we have our community in mind first and foremost. We stay busy in our community. It is a community of like minded people looking for like-minded people to join the cause of service for our Lord and Savior Jesus Christ and tarry until He comes.

Completed Tiny House.

Building A Ranch Yurt.

Inside of a Finished Yurt.

A Completed Yurt.

Rhonda's dad, John Alman and Husband, Jim Beyreis, Are Building The Ranch's Commercial Kitchen.

New Ranch Commercial Kitchen Built Using A Single-Wide.

Seedlings

Horsing Around. My Horse: Star (Front) and Blondie (back)

Ham Radio

Everyone Will Play Their Part. Attendees of First Ark of
Sustainability Retreat, 2021.

Michelle Hardesty Teaching About Natural Remedies at the 2021 Ark of Sustainability Retreat.

Bring It Back Home.

FINAL WORDS

During times of crisis we will still need cooks, gardeners, mechanics, builders, accountants, veterinarian, doctor or nurse, dentist, animal tender, homeschool teacher, social media connector, website manager. The community should be a wealth of resourceful people who have talents that complement one another. Kind of like a city outside of the city. The skills and needs are the same.

You need a board of directors for the community, rules to keep the community in order. Having a city outside of the city on open land with likeminded people can be the most peaceful feeling of freedom you can imagine.

Over 50 years ago the Hutterites taught me more than I could have ever imagined. They taught me more than I knew I would need to survive in this lifetime.

I am and will always be eternally grateful for that experience.

Today, we here at The Ark of Sustainability continue to build for the Lord. God has created space. The big kitchen is finished, the Greenhouses are up and some more are being built.

The seedlings are sprouting, and we are preparing for a new harvest. The tiny homes are complete, and the yurts are erected.

We are ready to serve.

God is still the still, small voice; can you hear Him?

I believe if my dad were still here, he would be very proud.

I hear the birds singing. Oh, there goes a bee that just landed on a flower. I take a deep breath in the air. So fresh.

It is a new day. And even with knowing what is on the horizon, being prepared makes me feel safe.

I hear the rumble of the community stirring on the brink of awakening…

Peace Be With You. Jim and Rhonda.

WOULD YOU LIKE TO ATTEND A FUTURE
ARK OF SUSTAINABILITY RETREAT?

Scan this code on your phone to visit our
website to learn more and register:

RHONDA IS AVAILABLE FOR SPEAKING!

Rhonda Beyreis is an engaging, funny and compelling professional keynote speaker, speaking on topics that include:

1. How to be Sustainable in Changing Times (Getting out of the City)
2. Protecting Your Greatest Assets When The End Hits
3. Central Bank Digital Currency
4. Preparing for the end of time
5. Smart cities/15 minute cities
6. Vegan Food. Friend or foe?

To book Rhonda for your conference, podcast, or event, contact:
Email: rhonda.beyreis@gmail.com
Call: 602.320.0100
Book Appointment: https://www.Calendly.com/gourmet-1/30min

ABOUT THE AUTHOR

Vegan Chef and Survivalist, Rhonda Beyreis hosts off-grid Living retreats on her 680-acre sustainable property where she teaches gardening, solar technology, firearm safety, natural  remedies, food preservation and off-grid living,

Beyreis' beliefs are that we all should be dependent-free from the government for our survival in these trying and uncertain times.

Beyond the realms of the United States of America, Rhonda has been seen and heard in the hearts of Guatemala, Philippines, Egypt, Tanzania, Ghana, Italy, and Zimbabwe, as a Humanitarian Medical Practitioner and Spiritual Food Speaker.

When not working her passion, you can find Rhonda donating her time to prison ministry to preach the Word and build platforms for Felons to obtain employment with ease.

As the Founder/CEO of RAWndalicious, Beyreis is a firm believer in: *"Let food be thy medicine and medicine thy food." – Hippocrates. A* graduate of the Living Light Culinary Institute, her goal is to create wholesome foods and teach others the value of healthy lifestyle choices that will benefit their overall well-being.

ALSO BY THE AUTHOR

COMFORT FOODS - VEGAN STYLE

https://www.rawndalicious.com/copy-of-recipes-1

REFERENCES

- Cabral, L. G. (2022, April 18). *Civil War Hardtack Recipe*. Delicious Cooks. https://www.deliciouscooks.info/civil-war-hardtack-recipe

- *Federal Reserve updates FedNow Service timing to mid-2023, marks beginning of full-scale pilot testing*. (n.d.). Board of Governors of the Federal Reserve System. https://www.federalreserve.gov/newsevents/pressreleases/other20220829a.htm

- Lisa. (2022). Water Glassing Eggs. *Farmhouse on Boone*. https://www.farmhouseonboone.com/water-glassing-eggs

- *Transforming our world: the 2030 Agenda for Sustainable Development | Department of Economic and Social Affairs*. (n.d.). https://sdgs.un.org/2030agenda

- ZenLedger. (2022). What Are Central Bank Digital Currencies (CBDCs)? *ZenLedger*. https://www.zenledger.io/blog/what-are-central-bank-digital-currencies-cbdcs